The Number Team have a Party

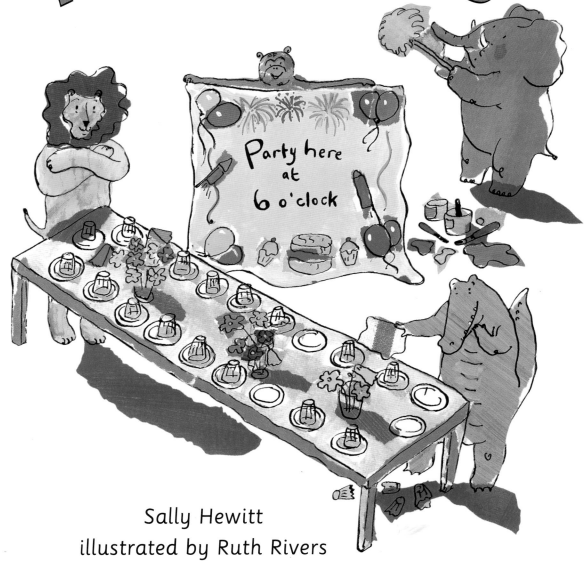

Party here
at
6 o'clock

Sally Hewitt

illustrated by Ruth Rivers

Thameside Press

Notes for parents and teachers
How to use this book

Each double page has a numeracy theme,
such as multiples, shapes, or telling the time.

The story

Question boxes

Monkey's
math tip

Question boxes

Each box has two questions. Elephant's questions
are easier than Crocodile's. Start with Elephant's
questions, then move on to Crocodile's. Or you
can choose to answer only Elephant's or only
Crocodile's questions. The answers are on page 30.

Monkey's math tip

Read Monkey's math tip for help with
the Number Team's questions, or extra
information about the math in the scene.

There are ideas for games
and activities on page 31.

How many different
shapes can you find?

Which shapes are
flat (2D) and which
are solid (3D)?

Shapes

Some solid shapes have
flat sides called faces.

Cube faces are squares.
Cuboid faces are rectangles.
A pyramid has 1 square face
and 4 triangular faces.

Meet the Number Team

Crocodile, Lion, Monkey, and Elephant
are throwing a party in the jungle—with
a feast, dancing, games, and fireworks.
They need your help to make sure
everything will be ready on time!

First the team delivers the party invitations. "Don't get lost," shouts Crocodile.

Follow the path to the banana trees.

Give Monkey directions to the banana trees.

Giving directions

When you give directions, it often helps to use a landmark. For example:
- Turn right at the signpost.
- Cross the river at the stepping stones.
- Turn left at the tall tree.

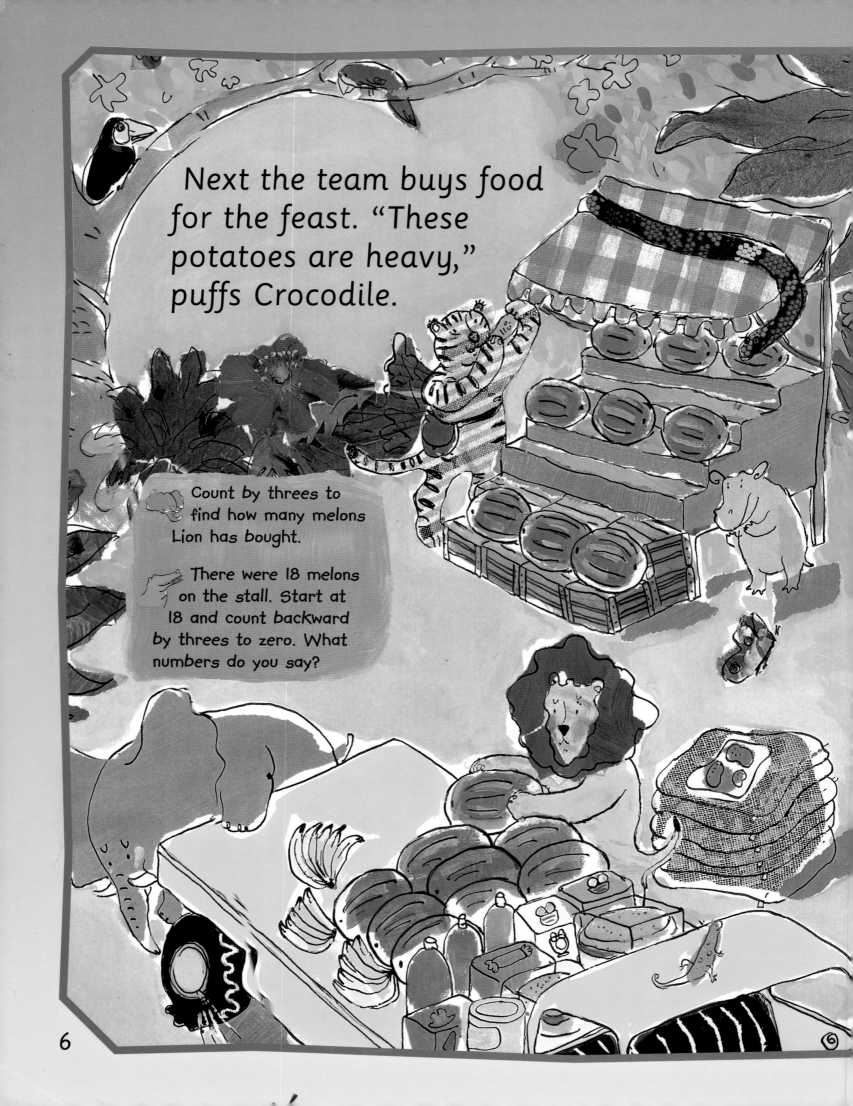

Next the team buys food for the feast. "These potatoes are heavy," puffs Crocodile.

Count by threes to find how many melons Lion has bought.

There were 18 melons on the stall. Start at 18 and count backward by threes to zero. What numbers do you say?

Count by fours to find how many coconuts Monkey has bought.

There were 20 coconuts on the stall to start with. Start at 20 and count backward by fours until you reach zero. What numbers do you say?

There are 10 potatoes in each bag. Count by tens to find how many potatoes Crocodile has bought.

Work out how many potatoes there were on the stall to start with if there are 10 potatoes in each bag.

Multiples

A multiple of 10 is a number that has been multiplied by 10. So 20, 30, 40, and 50 are all multiples of 10. All multiples of 10 end in 0.

Multiples of 5 end in 0 or 5.

Multiples of 2 end in 0, 2, 4, 6, or 8.

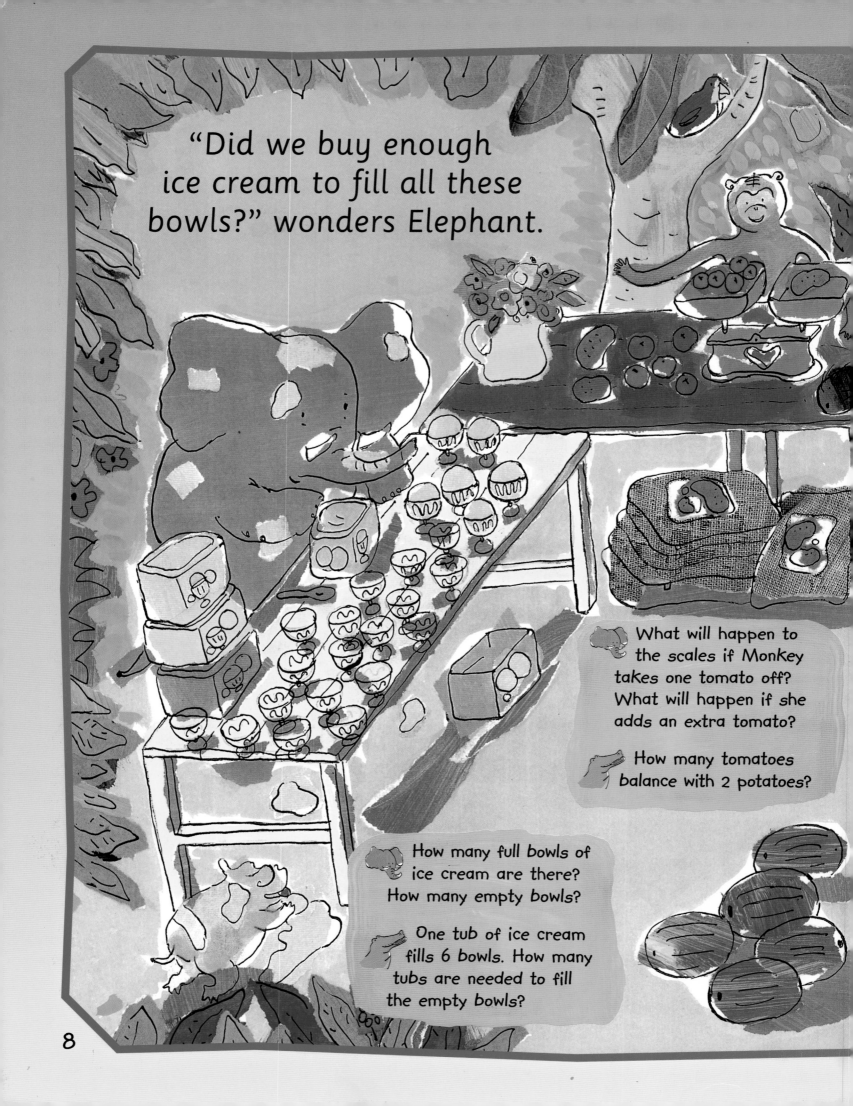

"Did we buy enough ice cream to fill all these bowls?" wonders Elephant.

What will happen to the scales if Monkey takes one tomato off? What will happen if she adds an extra tomato?

How many tomatoes balance with 2 potatoes?

How many full bowls of ice cream are there? How many empty bowls?

One tub of ice cream fills 6 bowls. How many tubs are needed to fill the empty bowls?

Which *bowl* holds the most icing? Which *bowl* holds the least icing?

Match each cake to a bowl that holds the right amount of icing to cover it.

Measuring

Liquids which you can pour, such as water, are measured in pints. There are 16 fluid ounces in 1 pint.

Solid things such as potatoes, sugar, or flour are measured in pounds. There are 16 ounces in 1 pound.

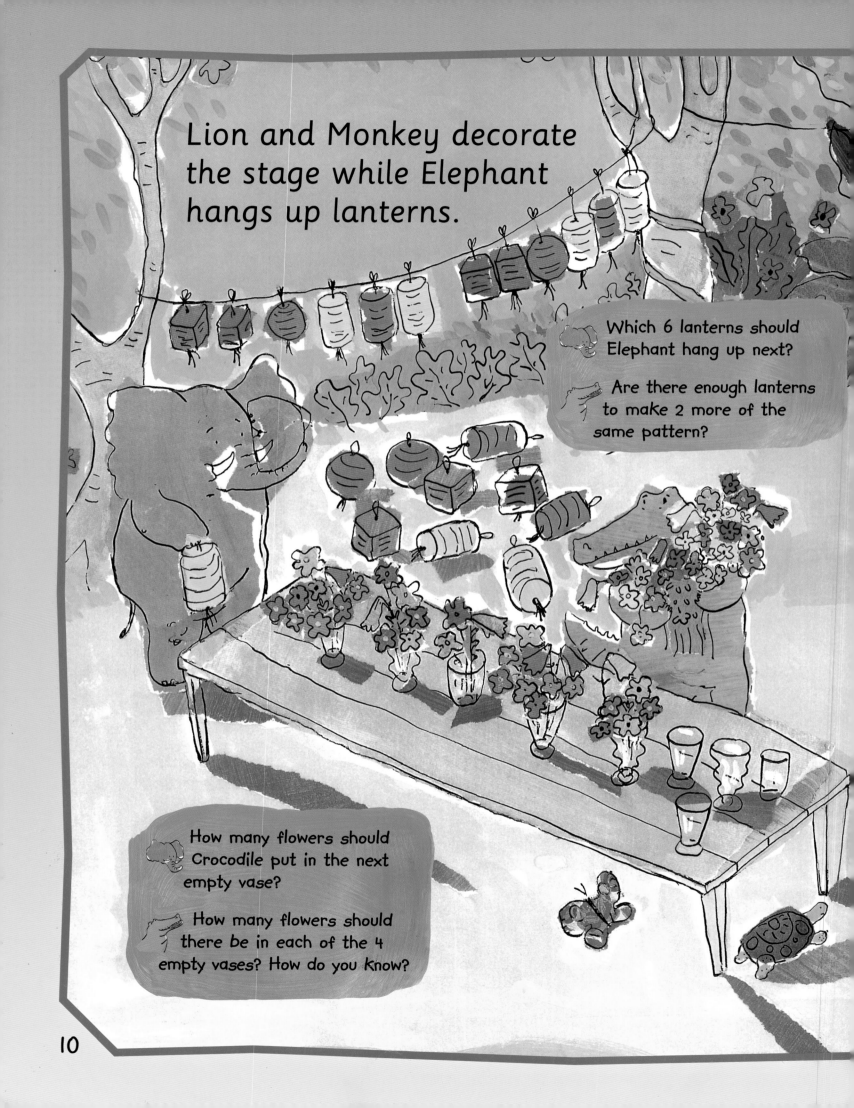

Lion and Monkey decorate the stage while Elephant hangs up lanterns.

Which 6 lanterns should Elephant hang up next?

Are there enough lanterns to make 2 more of the same pattern?

How many flowers should Crocodile put in the next empty vase?

How many flowers should there be in each of the 4 empty vases? How do you know?

How many balloons should Monkey put in the next bunch?

How many balloons should there be in the next 5 bunches? How do you know?

Patterns

You can use a number square to make interesting number patterns.

On a square with 100 numbers, count forward by twos. Color the numbers you land on. Do the same with fives and tens.

Then try counting forward by other numbers.

The band arrives as Crocodile checks his list. "Are all the musicians here?" he asks.

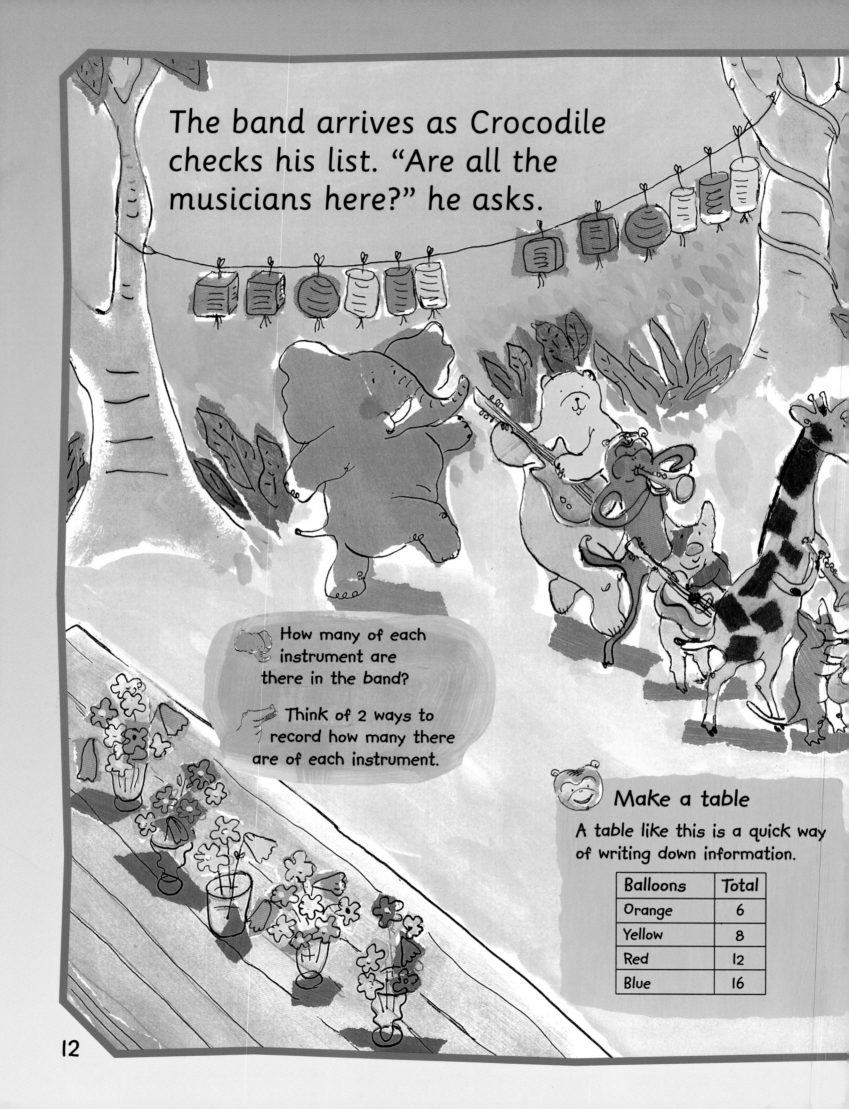

How many of each instrument are there in the band?

Think of 2 ways to record how many there are of each instrument.

Make a table

A table like this is a quick way of writing down information.

Balloons	Total
Orange	6
Yellow	8
Red	12
Blue	16

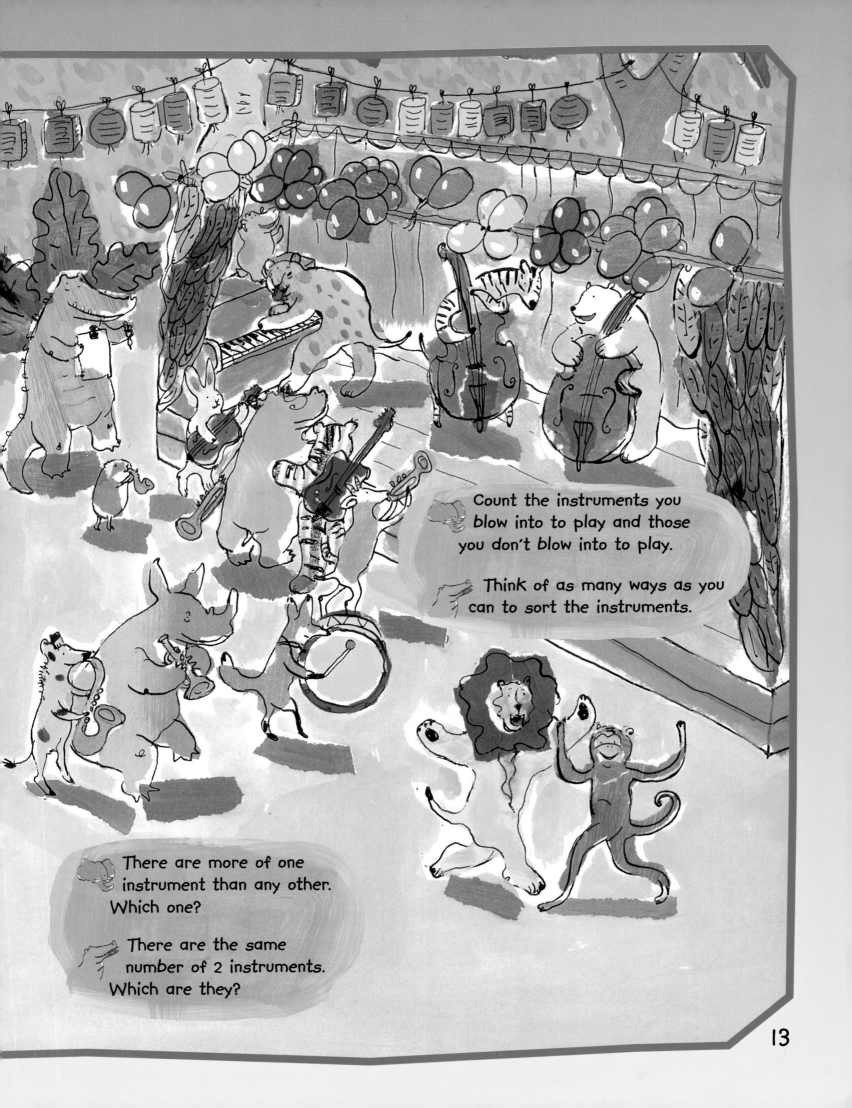

Count the instruments you blow into to play and those you don't blow into to play.

Think of as many ways as you can to sort the instruments.

There are more of one instrument than any other. Which one?

There are the same number of 2 instruments. Which are they?

"Hurry up, the party starts at 6 o'clock," shouts Crocodile.

Telling the time

Counting by fifteens helps you to tell the time.

There are 60 minutes in an hour.

15 minutes is a quarter of an hour.

30 minutes is half an hour.

45 minutes is three-quarters of an hour.

5:00

The animals start their jobs at different times. Who has the longest time to finish?

How long does everyone have to finish their jobs before the party starts?

5:15

5:30

Who has the shortest time to finish their job before the party starts?

How much more time than Lion does Crocodile have to finish his job?

5:45

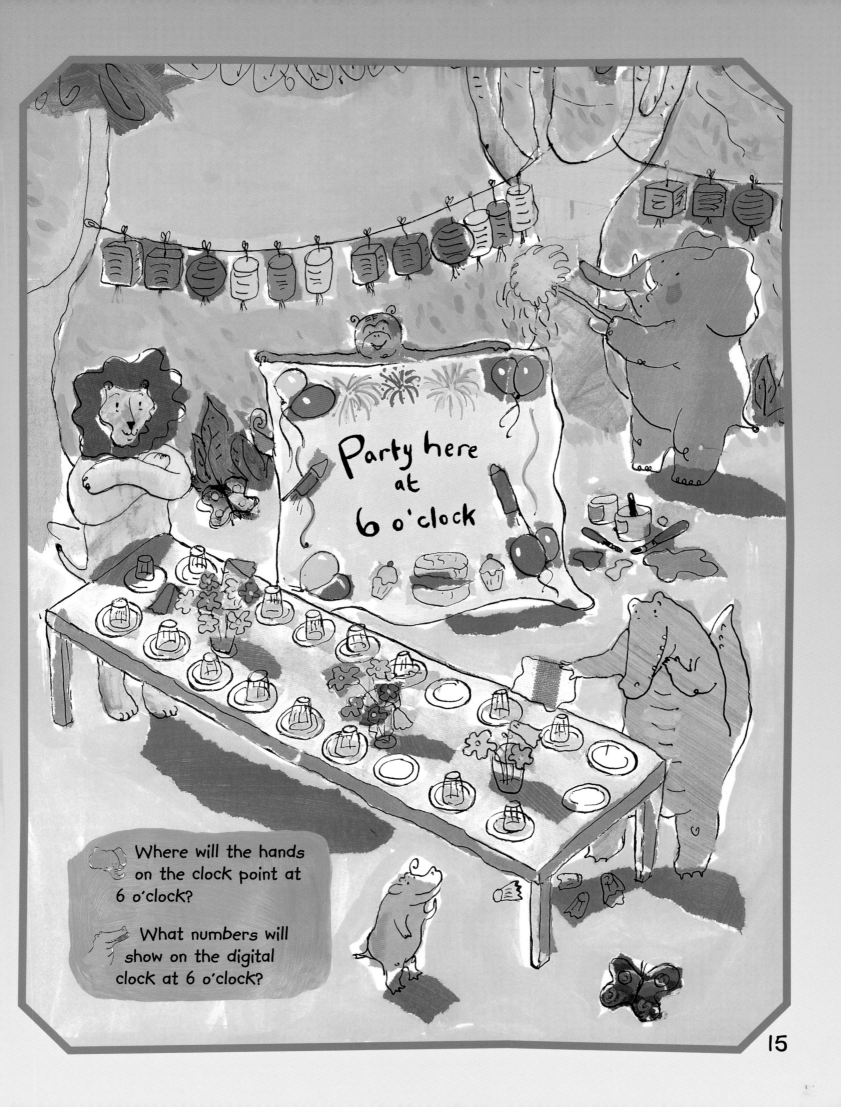

Party here
at
6 o'clock

Where will the hands on the clock point at 6 o'clock?

What numbers will show on the digital clock at 6 o'clock?

The guests arrive in a rush, from the tiniest turtle to the heaviest hippo.

Two chimps reach halfway to Giraffe's head. How many more are needed to reach the top?

How many more turtles are needed to make a line as long as Snake?

Find 3 animals taller than Ostrich. Find 3 which are shorter.

Find 3 animals you can describe as tall, taller, and tallest.

Measuring

When you measure how long, how wide, or how high something is, you need to use a ruler or a tape measure to be accurate. Usually when you use these, you measure in inches.

high

wide

long

Party here at **6** o'clock

Which bird's wingspan is the widest?

Find 3 birds whose wingspans are wide, wider, and widest.

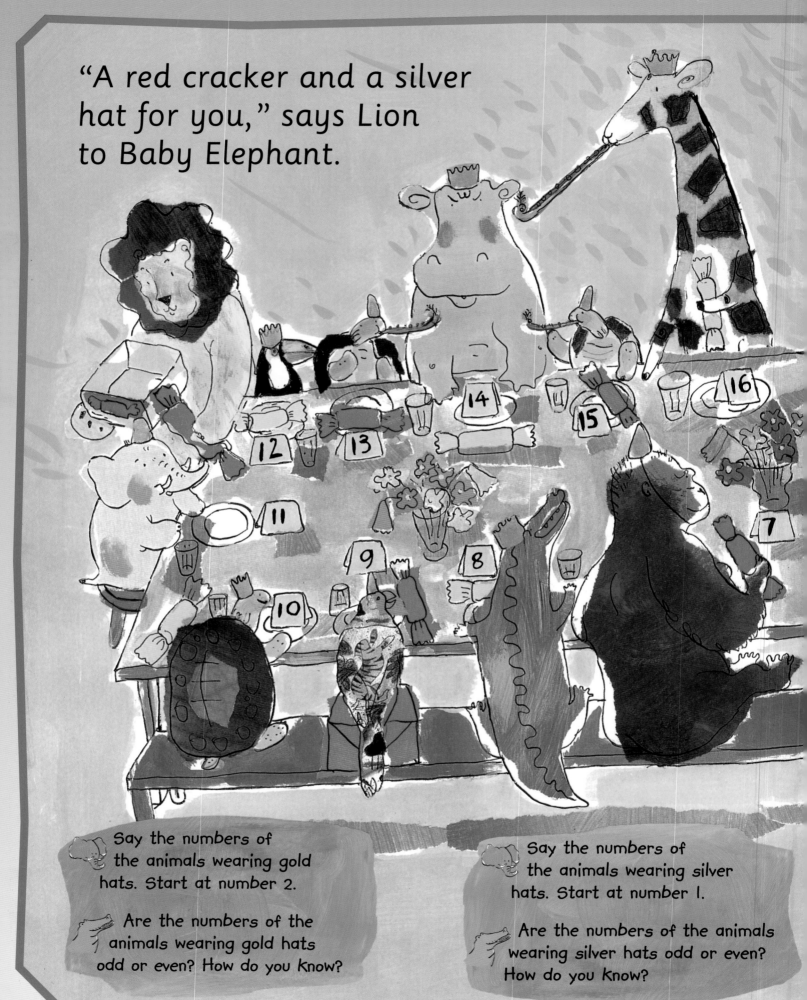

"A red cracker and a silver hat for you," says Lion to Baby Elephant.

Say the numbers of the animals wearing gold hats. Start at number 2.

Are the numbers of the animals wearing gold hats odd or even? How do you know?

Say the numbers of the animals wearing silver hats. Start at number 1.

Are the numbers of the animals wearing silver hats odd or even? How do you know?

Odd and even numbers

An even number divides exactly by 2. When an odd number is divided by 2, there is always 1 left over.

So 6 is an even number because it divides exactly by 2, into 3 and 3.

7 is an odd number because it does not divide exactly by 2—there is 1 left over.

Estimate whether the number of gold hats is the same as the number of silver hats.

Estimate whether the number of red crackers is the same as the number of yellow crackers. Count them to check if you were right.

19

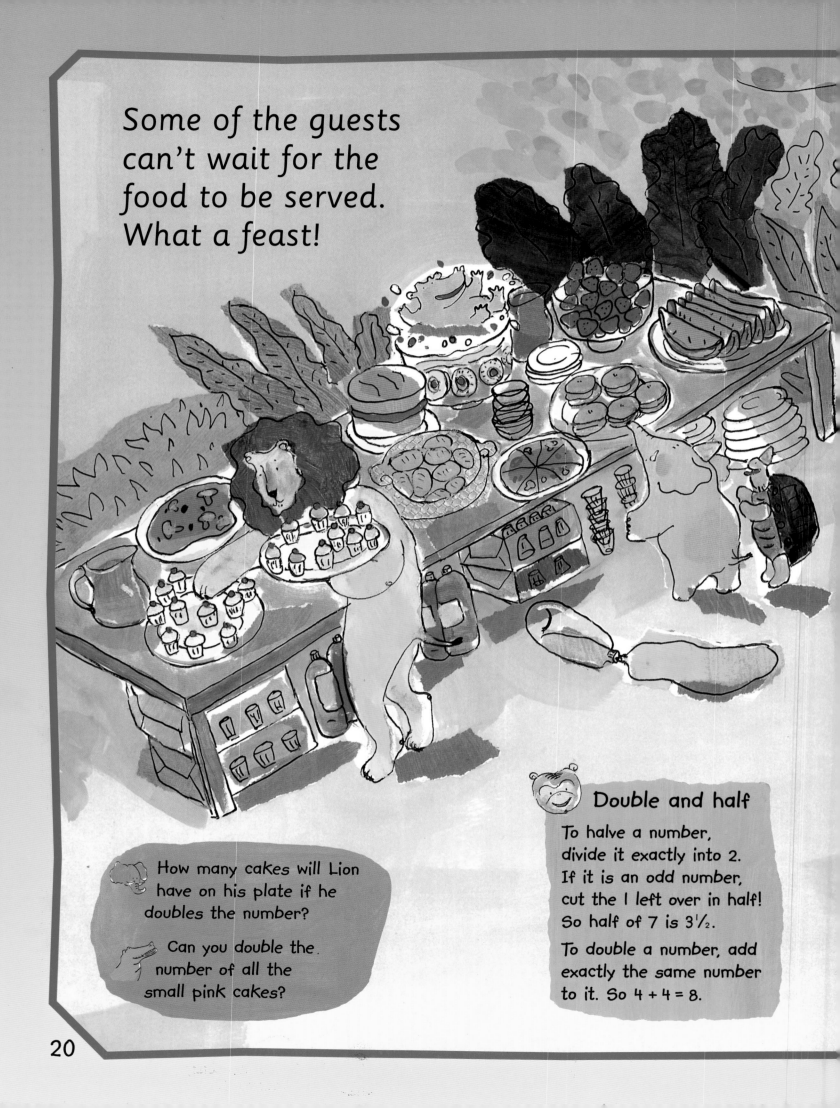

Some of the guests can't wait for the food to be served. What a feast!

How many cakes will Lion have on his plate if he doubles the number?

Can you double the number of all the small pink cakes?

Double and half

To halve a number, divide it exactly into 2. If it is an odd number, cut the 1 left over in half! So half of 7 is $3\frac{1}{2}$.

To double a number, add exactly the same number to it. So $4 + 4 = 8$.

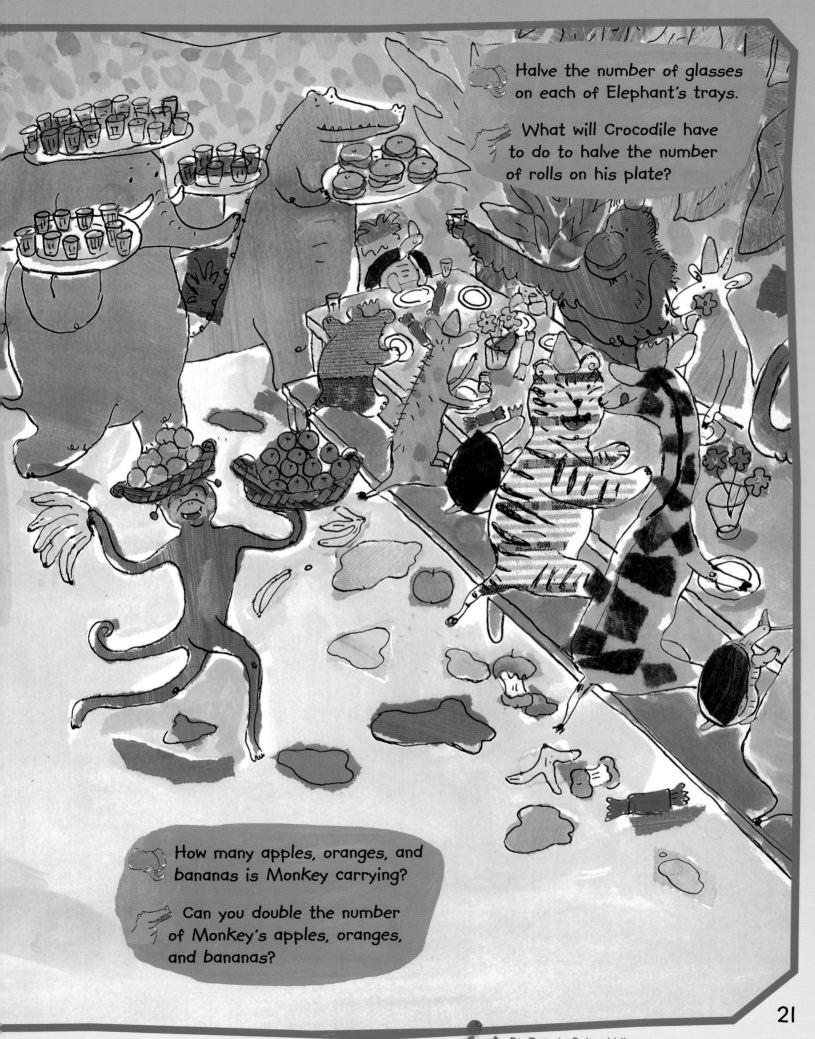

After tea, the animals blow bubbles and noisemakers, and pull crackers.

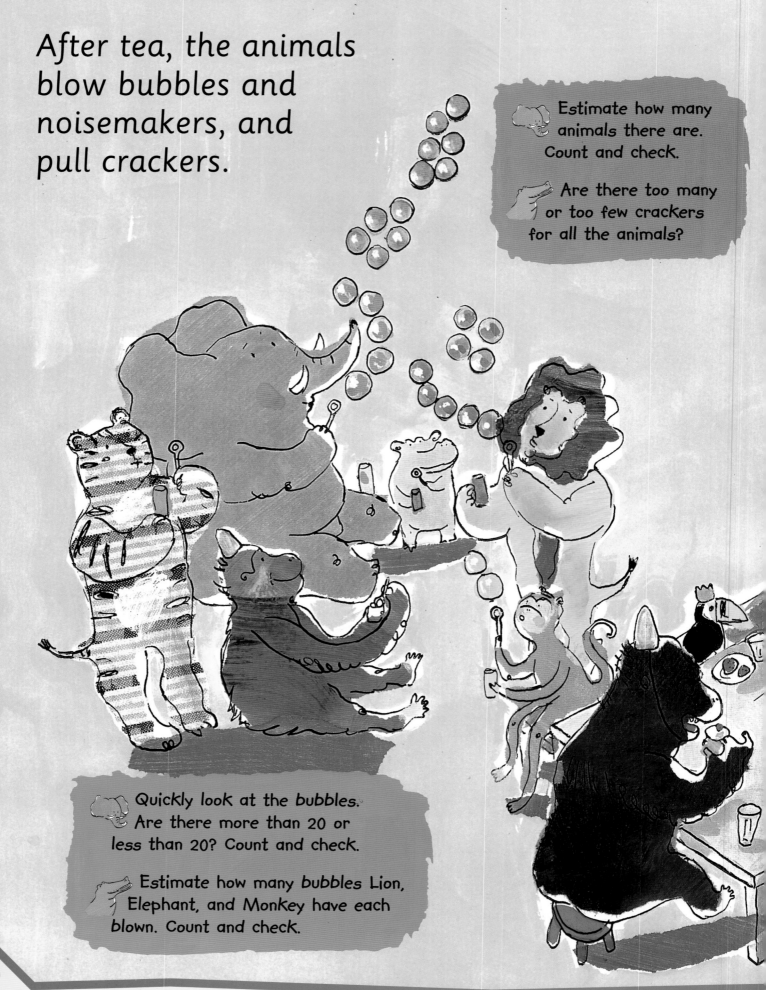

Estimate how many animals there are. Count and check.

Are there too many or too few crackers for all the animals?

Quickly look at the bubbles. Are there more than 20 or less than 20? Count and check.

Estimate how many bubbles Lion, Elephant, and Monkey have each blown. Count and check.

Quickly look at the apple cores. Estimate how many there are. Count and check.

Estimate how many there are of all kinds of things in the picture. How did you make your guess?

Estimating numbers

An estimate is a good guess. To estimate quite a big number of things, try to spot groups of numbers. For example, if there are 4 groups of 5 bubbles and about 3 floating on their own, you can guess about 20, but really there are 23.

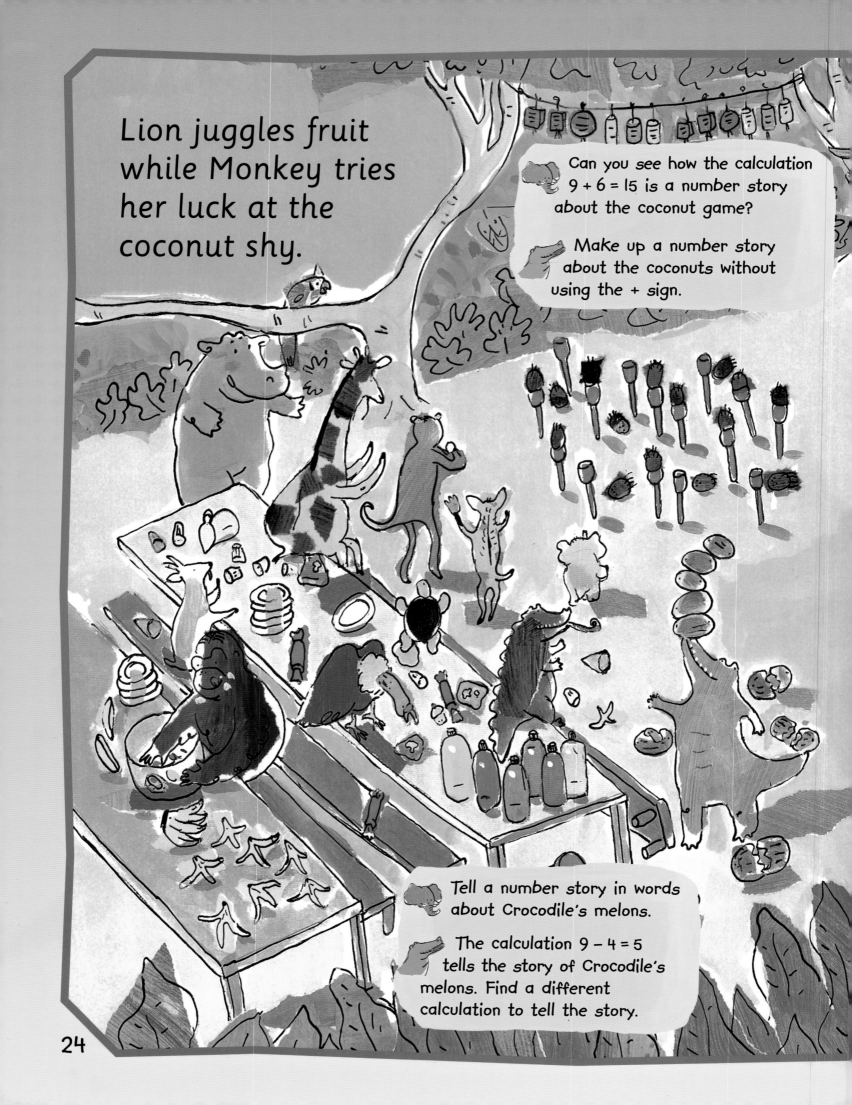

Lion juggles fruit while Monkey tries her luck at the coconut shy.

Can you see how the calculation 9 + 6 = 15 is a number story about the coconut game?

Make up a number story about the coconuts without using the + sign.

Tell a number story in words about Crocodile's melons.

The calculation 9 − 4 = 5 tells the story of Crocodile's melons. Find a different calculation to tell the story.

24

Make up a number story about the bananas and oranges that Lion is juggling.

Make up number stories from all sorts of things in the picture.

Number stories

A mathematical story uses numbers and symbols. A number story can be told in words. For example: Six turtles have jumped on Elephant. There are two waiting. This makes eight in total.

The calculation for this is 6 + 2 = 8.

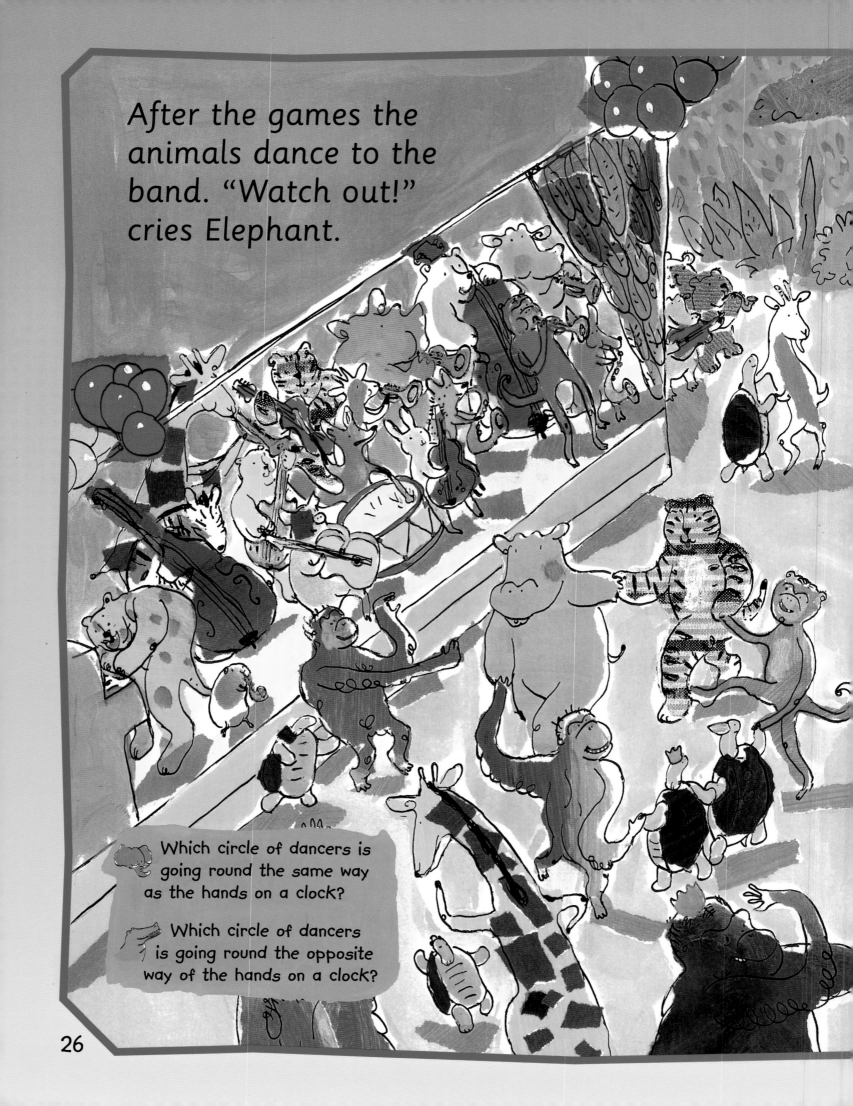

After the games the animals dance to the band. "Watch out!" cries Elephant.

Which circle of dancers is going round the same way as the hands on a clock?

Which circle of dancers is going round the opposite way of the hands on a clock?

26

Find a line of animals moving forward.

Find a line of animals moving backward.

Find the animal who is between Monkey and Hippo.

Give the position of an animal and ask a friend to guess which one it is.

Clockwise and counter-clockwise

If you are going around the same way as the hands on a clock, you are going clockwise. If you are going the opposite way, you are going counter-clockwise.

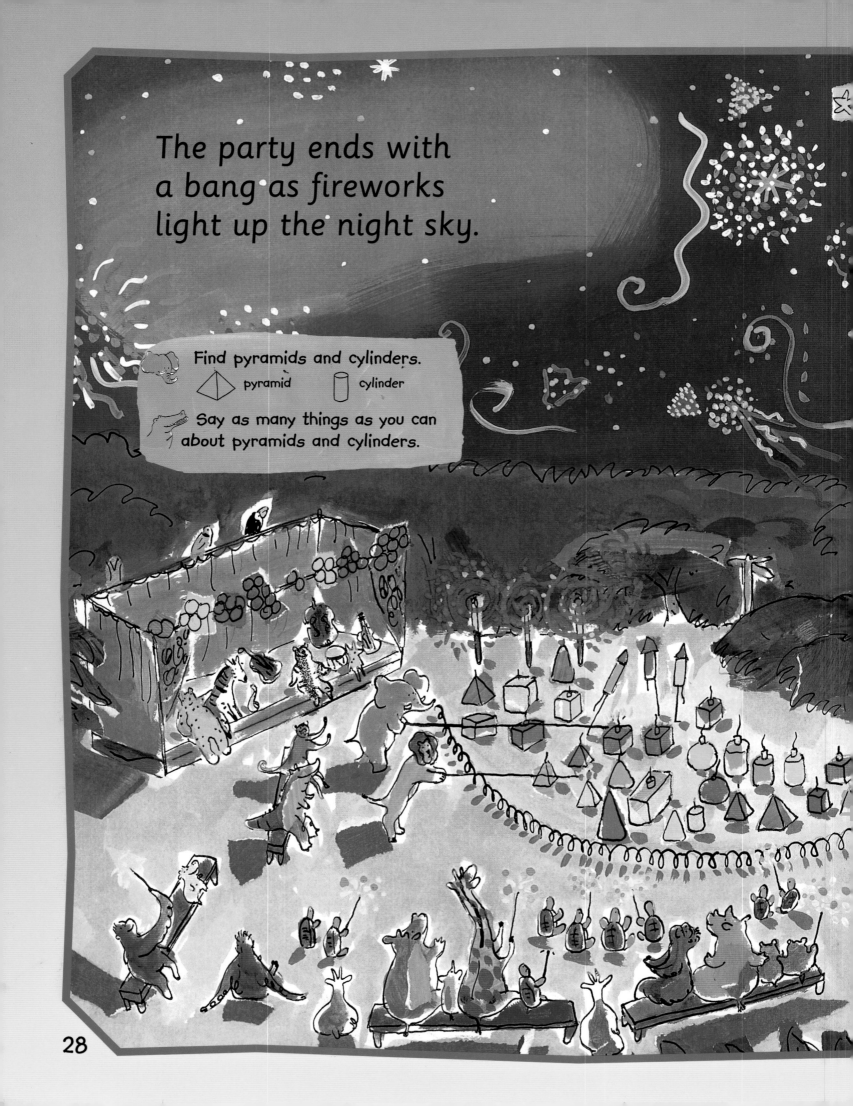

The party ends with
a bang as fireworks
light up the night sky.

Find pyramids and cylinders.

pyramid   cylinder

Say as many things as you can
about pyramids and cylinders.

Find spirals and stars.

spiral   star

Say as many things as you can about spirals and stars.

How many different shapes can you find?

Which shapes are flat (2D) and which are solid (3D)?

Shapes

Some solid shapes have flat sides called faces.

Cube faces are squares. Cuboid faces are rectangles. A pyramid has 1 square face and 4 triangular faces.

Answers

Elephant and Crocodile ask both open and closed questions. Closed questions have just one correct answer. Open questions have a number of different correct answers. These will encourage your child to think of alternative answers and, in some cases, to count all the different possibilities.

4–5 Giving directions

- See answer to Crocodile's question below.
- One route: right at signpost, left at pig, right at zebra, cross bridge, right at tall tree, straight on at signpost, then cross bridge.

- See answer to Crocodile's question below.
- One route: straight on at signpost, right at pink flowers, left at puddle, left at butterflies, left at turtle, cross bridge, then left at giraffe.

- One route: straight on at signpost, right at pink flowers, left at puddle, straight on at butterflies, over stepping stones, straight on at tall tree, then left at signpost.
- One route back for Monkey: cross bridge, go past signpost, straight on at tall tree, cross stepping stones, past butterflies, past puddle, left at flowers, then straight past signpost.

6–7 Multiples

- 9 melons.
- 18, 15, 12, 9, 6, 3, 0.

- 12 coconuts.
- 20, 16, 12, 8, 4, 0.

- 70 potatoes.
- 100 potatoes.

8–9 Weighing and capacity

- Taking away: the scales tip to the right. Adding: the scales tip to the left.
- 10 tomatoes.

- 6 full bowls. 18 empty bowls.
- 3 tubs of ice cream.

- The bowl of dark pink icing holds the most. The bowl of yellow icing holds the least.
- Dark pink bowl + cake next to Crocodile. Light pink bowl + cake next to green bowl. Green bowl + cake next to yellow bowl. Yellow bowl + cake to the right of dark pink bowl.

10–11 Patterns

- Orange cube, red cube, pink sphere, yellow cylinder, blue cylinder, yellow cylinder.
- No: 1 red cube, 1 yellow cylinder are missing.

- 3 flowers in the next vase.
- 3, 9, 6, and 3 flowers: because Crocodile is making a pattern counting backward by threes.

- 4 yellow balloons in the next bunch.
- 4, 6, 8, 2, and 4 balloons: the pattern is counting forward by twos, up to 8.

12–13 Sorting

- 4 guitars, 1 drum, 5 trumpets, 3 saxophones, 1 piano, and 2 double basses.
- You could write out a table (see Monkey's math tip). Or you could draw each instrument and write the numbers on the pictures.

- There are more trumpets (5).
- Drum and piano (1 of each).

- Blow into 8 (trumpets, saxophones). Don't blow into 8 (guitars, drum, piano, double basses).
- By color; whether they have strings; whether they are hit; whether they are carried.

14–15 Telling the time

- Elephant has the longest time (1 hour).
- Elephant: 1 hour. Crocodile: 45 minutes. Monkey: 30 minutes. Lion: 15 minutes.

- Lion (15 minutes).
- 30 minutes longer.

- Long hand points to 12, short hand to 6.
- 6:00.

16–17 Measuring

- 2 more chimps.
- 4 more turtles.

- Giraffe, Baby Giraffe, and Hippo are taller. Turtle, Goat, and Baby Hippo are shorter.
- Ostrich (tall), Baby Giraffe (taller), Giraffe (tallest).

- Eagle's wingspan is widest.
- Small Vulture (wide), Big Vulture (wider), Eagle (widest).

18–19 Odd and even numbers

- 2, 4, 6, 8, 10, 12, 14, 16, 18, 20.
- Even (the numbers divide exactly by 2).

- 1, 3, 5, 7, 9, 11, 13, 15, 17, 19.
- Odd (the numbers do not divide exactly by 2: there is always 1 left over).

- The same: 10 gold and 10 silver hats.
- The same: 10 red and 10 yellow crackers.

20–21 Double and half

- 20 cakes.
- 40 cakes.

- 8 gold, 5 green, 3 brown glasses.
- Cut one roll in half and take off 2½ rolls.

- 5 bananas, 8 apples, 12 oranges.
- 10 bananas, 16 apples, 24 oranges.

22–23 Estimate and check

- 20 animals.
- There are too few crackers (12).

- There are more than 20 bubbles (27 in all).
- Elephant 16, Lion 9, Monkey 2.

- 12 apple cores.
- 10 banana skins, 14 noisemakers, 8 bowls. Look out for groups to help you guess.

24–25 Number stories

- Nine coconuts are on their stands, six have been knocked off. That makes fifteen in all.
- 15 − 6 = 9.

- Crocodile is balancing five melons. Add four melons that he dropped, that makes nine.
- 5 + 4 = 9.

- Lion is juggling six oranges and three bananas. That makes nine pieces of fruit in all.
- One number story is: four animals are racing on balloons. Take away one balloon which has burst, to leave three balloons (4 − 1 = 3).

26–27 Position and direction

- The circle to the left of Crocodile.
- The circle in front of the stage.

- The line led by a turtle.
- The line with Elephant, a chimp, and a turtle.

- Tiger.
- One example: Lion is to the right of Giraffe.

28–29 Shapes

- Some of the fireworks on the ground are pyramids and cylinders.
- Pyramid: solid (3D); the base is a square; the other faces are triangles. Cylinder: solid (3D); 3 faces; 2 of the faces are circles of equal size.

- There are spirals and stars in the sky.
- Spiral: a flat (2D) curve that winds round and round. Star: flat (2D) shape; straight edges; a star can have any number of points.

- Pyramids, cubes, cuboids, cylinders, spheres, cones (all on the ground). Spirals, stars, circles, triangles, squares, diamonds (all in the sky).
- 2D: spiral, star, circle, square, triangle, diamond. 3D: pyramid, cube, cuboid, cylinder, sphere, cone.

Notes for parents and teachers
Games and activities

Use the Number Team's questions to help you find more math in the pictures. Then try these games and activities.

4–5 Giving directions

Draw a map of your journey from home to school. Give a friend directions from one place on the map to another. Can they follow the route on the map?

8–9 Weighing and capacity

Make hot chocolate for one person. In a mug, add 5 fl oz of hot (but not boiling) milk to 3 teaspoons of drinking chocolate, and stir until dissolved. How much milk and drinking chocolate are needed for 2, 3, or 4 people?

12–13 Sorting

Make some sandwiches for your friends. Find a way of recording information about what everyone wants, such as: wholemeal or white bread; cheese or peanut butter filling. Make the sandwiches to order.

14–15 Telling the time

Make a set of 24 blank cards. Choose 6 different times. Draw each time on 4 cards: on 2 cards draw a clock with hands, on one card a digital clock, and on the 4th write the time in words. Use them to play matching games.

18–19 Odd and even numbers

Fold a long strip of paper into a concertina. On the front fold draw a figure, with arms touching both edges. Cut it out to make a line of figures. Number them, using red for odd and blue for even numbers.

22–23 Guess and check

Put colored beads in a see-through plastic pot, draw a starry sky, or build a castle with wooden blocks. Ask friends to guess the number of beads, stars, or blocks. Who makes the most accurate guess?

26–27 Position

Hide treasures around a room. Write their position on cards —under a small table, behind the left drape, and so on. Friends take a card, find a treasure, then collect another card. How many treasures did each child find?

28–29 Shapes

Draw or paint a picture of a party, a fireworks display, or a carnival. See how many different 2D and 3D shapes you can include in your picture.

Distributed in the United States by
Smart Apple Media
1980 Lookout Drive
North Mankato, MN 56003

Text by Sally Hewitt
Illustrations by Ruth Rivers

Series editor: Mary-Jane Wilkins
Editor: Russell McLean
Designer: John Jamieson
Educational consultant: Norma Penny, Barnett
    Infants School, Chessington, Surrey, U.K.

ISBN 1-930643-63-2

Library of Congress Control Number: 2001088845

Printed in China

9 8 7 6 5 4 3 2 1

DATE DUE

NOV 1 '01			
JAN 31 '02			
FEB 13 '02			
FEB 28 '02			

DEMCO 38-296